Llama Beans

Compiled by **Charles Keller**

Illustrated by **Dennis Nolan**

Prentice-Hall, Inc.   Englewood Cliffs, New Jersey

Printed in the United States of America

Prentice-Hall International, Inc., London
Prentice-Hall of Australia, Pty. Ltd., North Sydney
Prentice-Hall of Canada, Ltd., Toronto
Prentice-Hall of India Private Ltd., New Delhi
Prentice-Hall of Japan, Inc., Tokyo
Prentice-Hall of Southeast Asia Pte. Ltd., Singapore
Whitehall Books Limited, Wellington, New Zealand

10 9 8 7 6 5 4 3 2 1

Library of Congress Cataloging in Publication Data

Keller, Charles.
  Llama beans.

  SUMMARY: A collection of jokes, riddles, and puns
about animals.

  1. Animals—Anecdotes, facetiae, satire, etc.
2. Wit and humor, Juvenile. [1. Animals—Anecdotes,
facetiae, satire, etc. 2. Jokes. 3. Riddles]
I. Nolan, Dennis   II. Title.
PN6231.A5K4   817'.5'408   78-14553
ISBN 0-13-539122-9

To Betharoonie

Books by Charles Keller

Ballpoint Bananas
Daffynitions
Giggle Puss
Glory, Glory, How Peculiar
Going Bananas
Laughing
Laugh Lines
Llama Beans
*The Little Witch Presents a Monster
    Joke Book*
More Ballpoint Bananas
The Nutty Joke Book
Punch Lines
School Daze
The Star-Spangled Banana
Too Funny for Words

What do llamas eat?

Llama beans.

Why did the farmer put bells
around the bull's neck?

Because his horns didn't work.

What did the beaver say to
the tree?

It's been nice gnawing you.

Where do cows go on Saturday
night?

To the moo-vies.

What do you call a cow that
sits down on the grass?

Ground beef.

How do you keep a turkey
in suspense?

I'll tell you tomorrow.

What do patriotic buffalos celebrate?

The bisontennial.

Who does a magician call when he loses his rabbit?

A hare restorer.

Why does a monkey scratch
himself?

He's the only one who knows
where it itches.

If a peacock loses his tail, where
does it get a new one?

At the retail store.

What do you get when you
pour boiling water down
the rabbit hole?

Hot cross bunnies.

What is horse sense?

Stable thinking.

What do you call a monkey
that eats potato chips?

A chip monk.

If you were chased by a hungry shark, what would you feed it?

Jawbreakers.

What do bees do with their honey?

They cell it.

What did the judge say when
the skunk walked into court?

Odor in the court.

When is a boy like a bear?

When he goes barefoot.

What does a mechanical
frog say?

Robot, robot.

Who performs operations at
the fish hospital?

The head sturgeon.

Why is a snake so smart?

Because you can't pull his leg.

Why is a fawn only worth 99 cents?

Because it's not old enough to be a buck.

Why are lobsters so greedy?

Because they are shellfish.

What do you call an
overweight lion?

The King Obese.

Why do elephants have trunks?

35

Because they don't have
glove compartments.

What do you call a lion who
crosses the Sahara Desert?

Sandy Claws.

What has two humps and is
found in Alaska?

A lost camel.

Why was the pony quiet?

Because he was a little horse.

What do you call a cow that
doesn't give milk?

An udder failure.

Why do zebras run in herds?

So they can get their
sneakers wholesale.

What do you get when you
cross a parrot with a
gorilla?

I don't know. But when
it talks, you listen.

What is the best year for a
kangaroo?

Leap year.